KU-271-469

Richard Scarry's
Best Counting
Book Ever

Willy Bunny has learned to count. After you read this book, you will be able to count, too. Then, see if you can add numbers, the way Willy has added them below for his parents.

$1+1=2$

$2+1=3$

$2+2=4$

$3+2=5$

$3 + 3 = 6$

$4 + 3 = 7$

$4 + 4 = 8$

$5 + 4 = 9$

$5 + 5 = 10$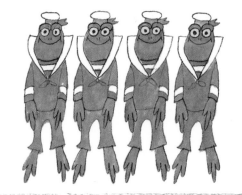

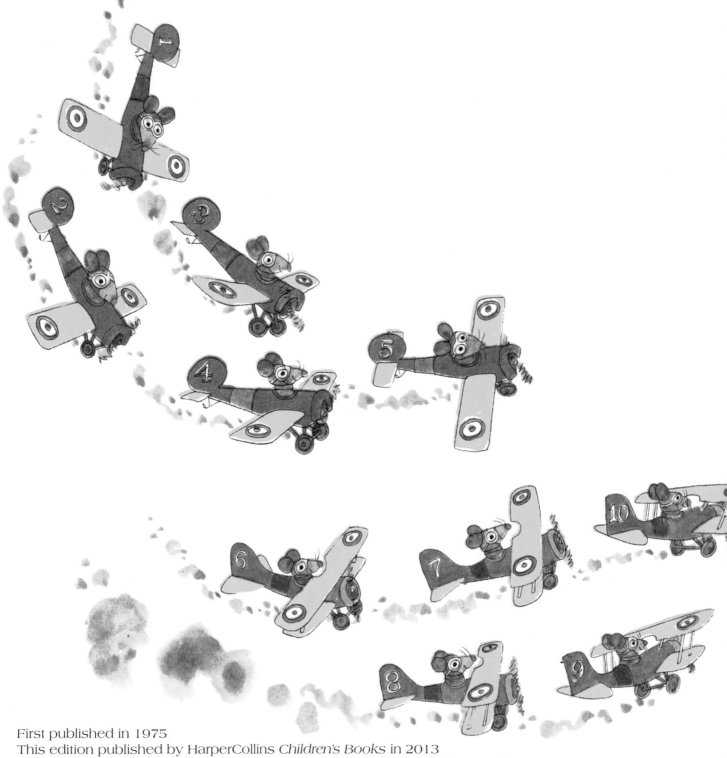

First published in 1975
This edition published by HarperCollins *Children's Books* in 2013
HarperCollins Children's Books is a division of HarperCollins *Publishers* Ltd,
77-85 Fulham Palace Road, London W6 8JB

1 3 5 7 9 10 8 6 4 2

ISBN: 978-0-00-793529 -1

© 1975 Richard Scarry Corporation

No part of this publication may be reproduced, stored in a retrieval system or transmitted in
any form or by any means, electronic, mechanical, photocopying, recording or otherwise,
without the prior permission of HarperCollins Publishers Ltd, 77-85 Fulham Palace Road,
London W6 8JB.

The HarperCollins website address is www.harpercollins.co.uk

Printed and bound in China.

Richard Scarry's
Best Counting Book Ever

HarperCollins *Children's Books*

"There is no one to play with,"
says Willy Bunny.
"What can I do?"

"Why don't you practise counting all
the things you see today?"
asks his father.
"Then at suppertime you can tell me
how many things you have counted."

"That sounds like fun," says Willy.
"I will start right now. I am *one* bunny and..."

1 one

"Oh, look! Here comes Sally Bunny. One bunny and one bunny make two bunnies."
Both bunnies have two eyes, two hands, two feet and two long ears.

2 two

One mother and one father make two parents. Two fried eggs make a good breakfast for Daddy.

Can you count two of anything else?

3 three

Willy and Sally go outside to play.
Along comes their friend, Freddy Bunny.
Two bunnies and one bunny make three bunnies.

How many wheels are on Freddy's tricycle?
That's right! There are three wheels.

"Look at the three trucks," says Willy.
"One is big and two are small."

4 four

Here comes Flossie Bunny with her wagon.
Three bunnies and one bunny make four bunnies.
Now there are two girl bunnies and two boy bunnies.
Flossie has brought four apples in her four-wheeled wagon for everyone to share.

Four mouse buses go down the street. Two are yellow and two are red.

5 five

Beep-beep. Here comes Joey on his go-cart.
That makes five bunnies. Four were here
already, and one more makes five.

Four of the bunnies hear their
mothers calling them home.
That leaves just one bunny – Willy.
But Willy doesn't mind being alone.
He still has lots of things to count.
He sees five racing cars.

"One, two, three,
four, five," he
counts.

6 six

Ding! Ding! Ding!

Ding! Ding! Ding!

Ding! Ding! Ding!

Five fire engines and a fire chief's
car are speeding down the street.
That makes six in the fleet.
Three have ladders. Three do not.
Five are red and one is white.
Where is the fire?

7 seven

The fire must be in the
Cat family's farmhouse.

Seven cats are running out of the house.
Five are dressed and ready for school.
The other two are a mother and a baby.

8 eight

The fire is in Mother Cat's oven,
where she is baking eight pies.
Five pies are burned,
but three are baked just right.
They did get a little wet, though.

How many cats are
going to eat at the table?

9 nine

Splish! Splosh! Splash!

Splish! Splosh! Splash!

Well, those firemen have certainly made
a mess of Mother Cat's kitchen floor.
Splish! Splosh! Splash!

They clean up with nine mops.
Five mops are red, two are green and two are yellow.

10 ten

Here comes Farmer Cat with ten
watermelons from his garden.
He slips and half of them fly out of his basket.

Five watermelons are
still safe in his basket.

Who has caught the sixth, seventh, eighth and ninth melons?

Will Mother Cat be able to catch the tenth one before it falls to the ground? Look out, Mother Cat!

Now let us see what Willy has counted so far.

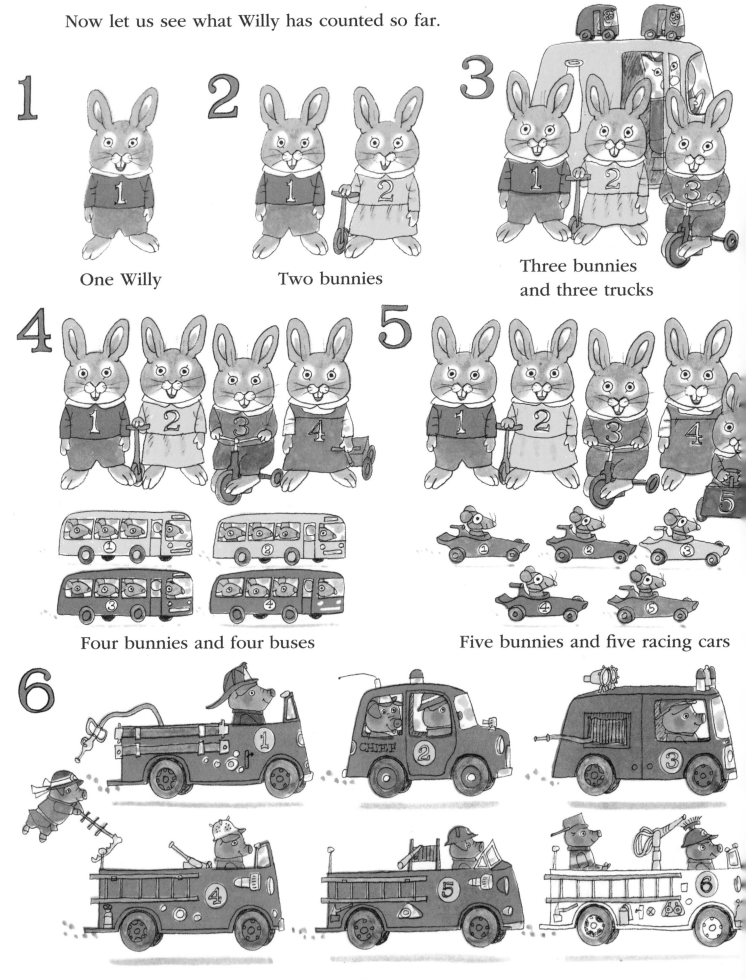

1 One Willy

2 Two bunnies

3 Three bunnies
and three trucks

4 Four bunnies and four buses

5 Five bunnies and five racing cars

6 Six fire engines

7 Seven cats

8 Eight pies

9 Nine mops

10 Nine melons, and the one that
Mother Cat caught, makes ten melons.
Good for her!

11 eleven

"Now I must find
some bigger numbers,"
says Willy.
"I will look around the farm
and see what I can find."

12 twelve

Farmer Cat goes into the hen
house to gather eggs.
He slips again and frightens
his twelve hens.

Five hens are red.

Mother Cat is trying to hang
eleven shirts on the line.
Five of them blow away in the strong
wind. Then five more blow away.
But Mother Cat grabs the eleventh shirt.

Five of them
are white.

And two more
are black.

Twelve hens in all.
They laid twelve eggs –
one dozen eggs!
Count them yourself.

13 thirteen

Willy says goodbye to Farmer Cat. As he walks down the lane he sees thirteen tractors in the field.

Five are ploughing.

Five are planting.

And three are just resting.

14 fourteen

Suddenly, Willy discovers fourteen travellers who have stopped to rest in the lane.

Five are sleeping.

Five are eating.

And four are playing a game.

Here! Here! Stop fighting over the cards, you rascals!

15 fifteen

A little further on, Willy hears fifteen musicians playing.

Oompah!
Oompah!

There are five tuba players.
Oompah! Oompah!

Oompah!
Oompah!

16 sixteen

Going past the railway yard, Willy sees a train made up of sixteen wagons.

Five are box wagons.

Five are coal wagons.

Tootle-tee-toot!

Five are trumpet players. ***Tootle-tee-toot!***

Can you count how many drummers there are?
Boom-da-da-boom!

Five are petrol wagons.

And one is a guard's van.

A little engine is going
to join up to the wagons.
Do you think it can
pull them all away?

17 seventeen

Suddenly, seventeen aeroplanes
swoop down on Willy.

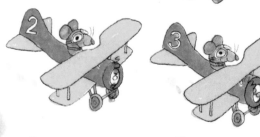

Five have single wings.

Five have double wings.

18 eighteen

A long car drives by with eighteen happy lions.
There are five gentleman lions and five lady lions
sitting in the front part of the car.

And two are jets.

Whooossssshhh!

Five have triple wings.

Five girl lions and three boy lions are
sitting in the back of the car.
That makes eighteen happy lions in all.

19 nineteen

Willy walks up to nineteen pigs having a picnic.

20 twenty

Twenty cats are playing football. Ten cats are on each team.

Just look at that long hotdog!
Do you think it is big enough to feed
nineteen very hungry pigs?

Look! Number
six has just
scored a goal.

30 thirty

Willy counts thirty children coming home from school.

He doesn't count the bus drivers. How many bus drivers are there?

SCHOOL BUS 5

SCHOOL BUS 10

SCHOOL BUS 15

40 forty

Forty mouse cars have engine trouble.
Four transporters are taking them to the
garage to be repaired.
My goodness! What a bumpy road!

50 fifty

As Willy walks down by the beach, he sees fifty boats out in the ocean.

There are five barges,

five sailboats,

five submarines,

and five motorboats.

It looks as if one motorboat is in trouble.

He sees five ocean liners,

five fishing boats,

five tugboats,

five police boats,

five fire boats,

and five rowing boats.

Hey, there, firemen!
Be careful where you
squirt that water!

Fifty boats in all!

60 sixty

A little further along the beach,
Willy sees sixty frogs enjoying themselves.

How many frogs are
playing ball?

How many fishing frogs are about to fall into the water?

How many frogs are riding in sailboats?

70 seventy

It is getting late.
On his way home, Willy stops
at the Bugs' flower garden, where
he counts seventy flowers.
Mr. Bug lets Willy pick a flower
to take home to his mother.
She will be very pleased.

80 eighty

Eighty workers hurry home from work. Some are walking, some are riding.
One of the workers is already at his front door.
Why, it's Daddy Bunny! Willy is greeting him at the door.

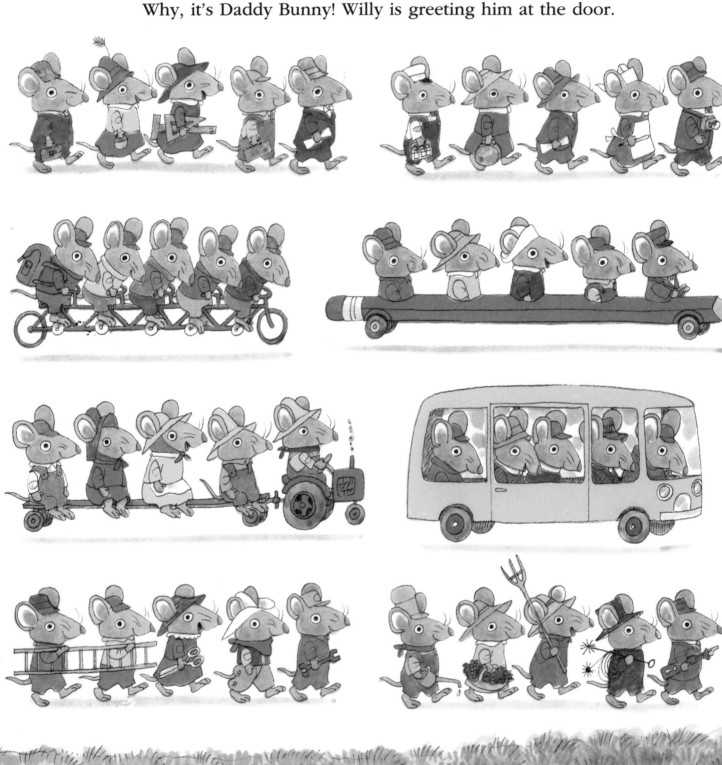

JOE'S HOT DOG FACTORY

90 ninety

At the supper table, Willy tells his father how many things he has counted during the day. Then the Bunny family begins to eat. They have ninety carrots for supper. My, what a hungry bunny family! Mmmm, those carrots taste good.

100 one hundred

After supper, Willy and his father go outside.
Willy counts one hundred fireflies glowing in the dark sky.
It looks as if the fireflies can count to one hundred, too.

And so can you!

Willy Bunny has learned to count.
Now you have read this book,
you can count, too.
Can you add numbers,
the way Willy has added them
for his parents?

$1 + 1 = 2$

$2 + 1 = 3$

$2 + 2 = 4$

$3 + 2 = 5$

3 + 3 = 6

4 + 3 = 7

4 + 4 = 8

5 + 4 = 9

5 + 5 = 10